HOCKEY SUPERSTARS

Paul Romanuk

Sixteen Super Mini-Posters of Top Hockey Stars
with Quotes and Facts and Useful Information
plus Your Own Record Keeper

Scholastic Canada Ltd.

Photo Credits

Daniel Alfredsson, Teemu Selanne © 1997 B. Bennett/Bruce Bennett Studios;
Pavel Bure © 1997 F. Howard/Protography;
Chris Chelios, Saku Koivu, Jarome Iginla ©1997 B. Wippert/Protography;
Wayne Gretzky © 1997 S. Babineau/Protography;
Jaromir Jagr (cover), Eric Lindros, Brendan Shanahan, Oleg Tverdovsky © 1997 J. McIsaac/Bruce Bennett Studios;
Peter Forsberg, Patrick Roy, Joe Sakic, John Vanbiesbrouck © 1997 R. Widner/Protography;
Mats Sundin © 1997 C. Andersen/Bruce Bennett Studios;
Doug Weight © 1997 J.Tremmel/ Bruce Bennett Studios.

ISBN 0-590-12401-3

Your Favorite Team — fill this part in at the beginning of the season.

Name of your favorite team: _Detroit Red Wings_

Conference: _Western_

Division: _Central_

Players on your favorite team at the start of the season

Number	Name	Position
5	Nicklas Lidstrom	Defence
14	Brendan Shanahen	Right wing
19	Steve Yzerman	Center
18	Kirk Maltby	Left wing
20	Martin LaPointe	Right wing
15	Mathieu Dandaneault	Left wing
08	Igor Larionav	Center
02	Vyachaslav Fetisov	Defence
17	Doug Brown	Right wing
25	Darren Mcarty	Left wing
27	Aaron Ward	Defence
4	Jamie Pusler	Defence
41	Brent Gilchrist	Left wing
30	Chris Osgood	Goalie
31	Kevin Hodson	Goalie
33	Kris Draper	Center
44	Anders Eriksson	Defence
3	Bob Rouse	Defence
26	Joey Kocur	Right Wing
13	Vyachaslav Kozla	Right wing

Changes, Trades, New Players

Fill this section in any time during the season. Use this space to write the names of players who join your team after the start of the season:

Yan Gulohouski - called up

_____

_____

_____

I. The Team Standings

Circle the team you think will finish in first place in each of the four NHL Divisions.

Western Conference

Pacific Division

Anaheim Mighty Ducks
Calgary Flames
(Colorado Avalanche)
Edmonton Oilers
Los Angeles Kings
San Jose Sharks
Vancouver Canucks

Central Division

Chicago Blackhawks
(Dallas Stars)
Detroit Red Wings
Phoenix Coyotes
St. Louis Blues
Toronto Maple Leafs

Eastern Conference

Atlantic Division

Florida Panthers
New Jersey Devils
New York Islanders
New York Rangers
(Philadelphia Flyers)
Tampa Bay Lightning
Washington Capitals

Northeast Division

Boston Bruins
Buffalo Sabres
Hartford Whalers
Montreal Canadiens
Ottawa Senators
(Pittsburgh Penguins)

II. The Playoffs

Which two teams will meet in the Stanley Cup Final?

Western Conference Winner:

Detroit

Eastern Conference Winner:

New Jersey

III. Stanley Cup Final

Which team will win the Stanley Cup?

Detroit

Your Team — All Season Long

You can keep track of your team's record all season.

The standings of hockey teams are listed on the sports page of the newspaper all season long. The standings will show you which team is in first place, second place, etc., right down to last place.

Some of the abbreviations you will become familiar with are: GP for games played; W for wins; L for losses; T for ties; PTS for points; A for assists; G for goals.

Check the standings on the same day of every month and copy down what they say about your team. By keeping track of your team in this manner you will be able to see when it was playing well and when it wasn't.

Your team: _Detroit Redwings_ ————————— month by month

(put the name of your team here)

DATE	GP	W	L	T	PTS
OCTOBER 1					
NOVEMBER 1					
DECEMBER 1					
JANUARY 1					
FEBRUARY 1					
MARCH 1					
APRIL 1					

Final Standings

At the end of the season print the final record of your team below:

Your Team	GP	W	L	T	PTS

Your Favorite Players' Scoring Records

While you're keeping track of your favorite team during the season, you can also follow the progress of your favorite players. Just fill in their point totals at the start of each month. The abbreviation for points is PTS.

PLAYER	OCT 1	NOV 1	DEC 1	JAN 1	FEB 1	MAR 1	APR 1

Your Favorite Goaltenders' Records

You can keep track of your favorite goaltenders' averages during the season. Just fill in the information below.

GAA is the abbreviation for Goals-Against Average. That is the average number of goals given up by a goaltender during a game over the course of the season.

PLAYER	OCT 1	NOV 1	DEC 1	JAN 1	FEB 1	MAR 1	APR 1

Leading Scorers and Goaltenders

At the end of the season you can get the final statistics for your favorite players and the rest of the league.

Fill in the leading scorer and the leading goaltender after the season is over.

NHL Leading Scorer	GP	G	A	PTS

NHL Leading Goaltender	GP	W	L	T	SO	GAA

Your All-Star Picks

Every year at the end of the hockey season, the Professional Hockey Writers Association selects the NHL's First and Second All-Star Teams. Here's a chance for you to make your selections. Remember to pick a player for every position.

First Team

Goaltender:_____

Left Defence:_____

Right Defence:_____

Center:_____

Left Wing:_____

Right Wing:_____

Second Team

Goaltender:_____

Left Defence:_____

Right Defence:_____

Center:_____

Left Wing:_____

Right Wing:_____

The list of the winners will be printed in the newspaper at the end of the season. Tape the list here. How many of your picks are on the team?

DANIEL ALFREDSSON
Ottawa Senators

The Ottawa Senators roster is the envy of many other NHL teams. A wealth of promising young athletes, like Alexei Yashin, Wade Redden, Alexandre Daigle and newcomer Daniel Alfredsson, are steering a course for the team's success. And they're on the right track: Ottawa set franchise records for wins and points last season and made the first round of the playoffs for the first time in their history.

As coach Jacques Martin points out, the key is effort. "We have to go out and work hard every night," he says. "That's a tough thing to do over an 82-game season, but that's what will make the difference between a team winning the close games and losing them."

Something else that makes a difference is talent — like Daniel Alfredsson's. His arrival on the scene has had a major impact on the Senators.

As rookies go, Daniel was seasoned. Drafted by the team at 21, Daniel was older than most draft picks. And before joining Ottawa he played another full season with Vastras Frolunda in the Swedish Elite League.

The extra experience seemed to jump-start Daniel's NHL career. Two years ago he led his team — and all rookies — in scoring, with 26 goals and 35 assists. He topped it off by winning the 1996 Calder Memorial Trophy as the top NHL rookie.

"It was such a big honor to win the award," says Daniel. "You dream about playing in the NHL, but to win the Calder Trophy just made it seem all that much more like a dream. It is something I will never forget."

While he enjoys offensive hockey best, Daniel knows the importance of being versatile. "Of course it is the most fun to score goals, but I also realize that a team must play good defence to win games," he says.

Hard work, talent, experience, versatility — have the Ottawa Senators found the recipe for success?

STATS
Daniel Alfredsson

- Ottawa's 5th pick (133rd overall) 1994 NHL Entry Draft
- First NHL Team & Season — Ottawa Senators 1995–96
- Born — December 11, 1972, in Grums, Sweden
- Position — Right Wing
- Shoots — Right
- Height — 1.80 m (5'11")
- Weight — 84 kg (187 lbs.)

Daniel Alfredsson

Right Wing
Ottawa Senators

PAVEL BURE
Vancouver Canucks

Pavel Bure is in select company. Twice in his career, he's scored 60 goals in a single season. Only eight others have managed to equal or better that record, among them Wayne Gretzky, Mario Lemieux and Brett Hull. But since those two seasons, 1992–1993 and 1993–1994, it's been tough going for the "Russian Rocket."

First, Pavel finished with only 20 goals during the shortened 1994–1995 lockout season. The next season saw him fall farther behind: after 15 games he suffered a severe knee injury. Last season he finished with 23 goals and 32 assists for 55 points — an improvement, but still nowhere close to his former successes.

"I knew it would be tough coming back from the knee injury," said Pavel. "I knew the fans and my teammates were counting on me. But it was difficult, because I hadn't played a full season in two years. No matter how much you practice and rehab, it still isn't the same as being in a game. The timing and everything is very different."

Being away from the game made Pavel realize how easy it is to take a hockey career for granted.

"I know that sometimes when you're playing you complain that you play too many games or that you're tired," he says. "[But] when I had to practice alone for six months, I appreciated how exciting it is to go on the ice with 18,000 people cheering for you."

What really draws the cheers from Pavel's fans is his blinding speed. When he flies down his wing with the puck, there are few players — if any — who can stay with him. In fact, the biggest challenge for his past coaches has been finding linemates quick enough to keep up with him!

"Pavel is one of those players who make you jump out of your seat," says Vancouver coach Tom Renney. "There are still times when he does things that just make you shake your head in amazement."

It may have taken a season for Pavel to return to his old self on the ice, but now he's poised to bring Canucks fans to their feet again.

STATS
Pavel Bure

- Vancouver's 4th pick (113th overall) 1989 NHL Entry Draft
- First NHL Team & Season — Vancouver Canucks 1991–92
- Born — March 31, 1971 in Moscow, Russia
- Position — Right Wing
- Shoots — Left
- Height — 1.78 m (5'10")
- Weight — 85 kg (189 lbs.)

PAVEL BURE

Right Wing
VANCOUVER CANUCKS

CHRIS CHELIOS
Chicago Blackhawks

Some things never change for Chris Chelios. Whenever he heads to a hockey rink he is reminded of how much he loves to play the game.

"For me, it can be a little thing like the smell of the rink or walking into the building," he says. "Once I'm on the ice nothing bothers me — I just love the game and I enjoy playing. It still feels like it did when I was ten or eleven."

A Chicago native, Chris still remembers how it felt to sit in the old Stadium with his dad, watching Blackhawks legends like Bobby Hull, Stan Makita, Bill White and Tony Esposito.

"I think it helps to still have the kind of enthusiasm for the game I had when I was a kid," he says. "It helps to keep me sharp. I wish more guys still felt that way. It's tough now because we all have so many outside interests away from the game. You have to remind yourself not to get away from team concepts because that's what the sport is all about — enthusiasm and wanting to do things as a team."

On his own, Chris has won the James Norris Trophy for best NHL defenceman several times, and he's played in the All-Star Game eight times. There is simply no defenceman in hockey who plays as hard as Chris does. At home or on the road, fans count on him to play with an intensity that makes his opponents wary.

Still, as great an individual player as he is, he is most satisfied by his team successes, like Montreal's Stanley Cup win in 1986, and more recently, the USA's victory over Canada in the 1996 World Cup final.

"That was a great win for us, with a great group of guys," recalls Chris. "I was proud to be an American and I think it did a lot for our sport in the US. I'm proud of what I've done as an individual in my career, but being part of a winning team like this is a feeling that can't be beat."

If Chris's winning spirit catches on, the Blackhawks will be hard to beat.

STATS
Chris Chelios

- Montreal's 5th pick (40th overall) 1981 NHL Entry Draft
- First NHL Team & Season — Montreal Canadiens 1983–84
- Born — January 25, 1962, in Chicago, Illinois
- Position — Defence
- Shoots — Right
- Height — 1.85 m (6'1")
- Weight — 84 kg (186 lbs.)

CHRIS CHELIOS

Defence
CHICAGO BLACKHAWKS

PETER FORSBERG
Colorado Avalanche

Peter Forsberg has been playing hockey nearly all his life. He started playing at about five years old, on an outdoor rink near his home in Ornskoldsvik, Sweden.

As Peter got older and his playing improved, he would envision himself as Hakan Loob — a Swedish star who played with the Calgary Flames from 1983 to 1989.

"He was my idol," he says. "He was an awesome player in Sweden before he left to play in the NHL. The way he could skate and shoot the puck. . . ."

Now, at the age of 24, Peter is one of the world's best players.

"He is a hero, for sure," says Swedish hockey veteran Anders Hedberg. "He was a big star before he ever played in the NHL. When Peter scored the winning goal for Sweden in the 1994 Olympics it was one of the greatest moments in Swedish hockey history."

Peter's triumphant moment, in a shootout with Canada for the gold medal, was immortalized on a Swedish postage stamp. Fans at home refer to it as "The Stamp Goal."

Since then, Peter has put his stamp on the NHL. He won the Calder Trophy in 1994–1995 and helped Colorado clinch its first Stanley Cup in 1996. Despite missing 17 games last year, he still led his team in scoring with 86 points. His colleagues consider him one of the strongest two-way players in the game.

"He is definitely one of the most complete players I have ever seen," says his teammate Joe Sakic. "He's good in both ends of the ice with the puck and without it. He's also a very unselfish player."

"I enjoy a good pass as much as I do scoring a nice goal," says Peter. "With our team there is usually someone open for me to pass the puck to. If not, then I will try to go to the net. Sometimes you have to be patient."

Peter's good sportsmanship makes him an ideal role model for kids. And no doubt, on rinks all over Sweden, a whole new generation of young players is pretending to be him.

STATS
Peter Forsberg

- Philadelphia's 1st pick (6th overall) 1991 NHL Entry Draft
- First NHL Team & Season — Quebec Nordiques 1994–95
- Born — July 20, 1973, in Ornskoldsvik, Sweden
- Position — Center
- Shoots — Left
- Height — 1.83 m (6')
- Weight — 85.5 kg (190 lb.)

PETER FORSBERG

Center
COLORADO AVALANCHE

WAYNE GRETZKY
New York Rangers

There is nothing like a little doubt to bring out the best in an elite athlete.

Despite all he has done in the game, Wayne Gretzky was confronted with doubters as he headed into last season. Many felt Gretzky had fallen behind, that his days of making a major contribution to a team were over.

"I heard the talk," says Wayne. "I just decided to go out and prove people wrong. I was very determined at the start of the season to go out and put the season before behind me — to have fun and really help this team."

The 1995–1996 season was not a happy one for Wayne. He was playing for a deteriorating team in Los Angeles; then, after months of trade talk, he was shipped to St. Louis. Things got more complicated there, as he was unable to come to a contract agreement with the Blues. He finally became a free agent and signed with the New York Rangers.

"The whole situation — the trade, the ongoing contract talks — it was really stressful for me and others around me," says Wayne. "It couldn't help but have an effect on the way I played the game. [But] last season was a great turnaround. I was having fun again."

Wayne reached yet another major milestone last season, scoring his 900th career regular-season goal. It happened February 21, in the second period of a 7–2 loss to the Hartford Whalers.

This season, Wayne is looking forward to his chance to represent Canada at Nagano, Japan. For the first time in its history, the NHL is shutting down its regular-season schedule to allow players to participate in the Olympic Winter Games.

"I've said all along that it would be a dream to play at the Olympics for Canada," says Wayne. "If I'm given the chance to play, I believe I can contribute. I don't want to be there because of what I've done. I'd like to be there because I can still do things that help a team to be successful."

Wayne still has plenty of drive left in him, and this year he'll have another chance to prove the doubters wrong.

STATS
Wayne Gretzky

- Reclaimed by Edmonton prior to June 1979 Expansion Draft
- First NHL Team & Season — Edmonton Oilers 1979–80
- Born — January 26, 1961, in Brantford, Ontario
- Position — Center
- Shoots — Left
- Height — 1.83 m (6')
- Weight — 81 kg (180 lbs.)

WAYNE GRETZKY

Center
NEW YORK RANGERS

Jarome Iginla
Calgary Flames

The timing couldn't have been better. A year before Jarome Iginla arrived on the NHL scene, he had been drafted by the Dallas Stars, preparing to play for Canada in the World Junior Hockey Championships. Then, just before the start of the tournament, he was told he'd been traded to the Calgary Flames.

The tough part for him was that the Flames had just traded *away* one of their most popular players, Joe Nieuwendyk. Calgary fans were unhappy — most felt the team had just given away a star for an unknown player.

But Jarome quickly changed their minds — he went out and played incredible hockey at the tournament. Canada won the gold medal and Jarome was named Most Outstanding Forward, with five goals and seven assists to his credit.

What was his secret?

"I tried not to think about the trade too much," says Jarome. "I just wanted to go out and help Canada win the gold. I guess, looking back, the timing was pretty good, though. Maybe it made people who hadn't heard of me or seen me play before take some notice."

"We knew what Jarome was capable of long before we made the trade," says Calgary general manager Al Coates. "I know the initial reaction from a lot of the fans was 'Joe who?' but we knew the guy, and people in our organization spoke highly of him both as a player and a person."

One of Jarome's greatest qualities on ice is his ability to handle the puck, even in the corners and along the boards at the opponents' end. These are trouble spots for many players, especially when the opposing team starts to close in. But Jarome maneuvers beautifully.

"There is no question he's a great talent," says Flames coach Pierre Page. "He makes plays sometimes that just make you shake your head because you can't believe he's only been in the league for one season. He thinks out there very well for a young player. He's smart off the ice, too."

Surely this season, Calgary fans will be sitting up and taking notice of their newest rising star.

STATS
Jarome Iginla

- Dallas's 1st pick (11th overall) 1995 NHL Entry Draft
- First NHL Team & Season — Calgary Flames 1996–97
- Born — July 1, 1977, in Edmonton, Alberta
- Position — Right Wing
- Shoots — Right
- Height — 1.85 m (6'1")
- Weight — 87 kg (193 lbs.)

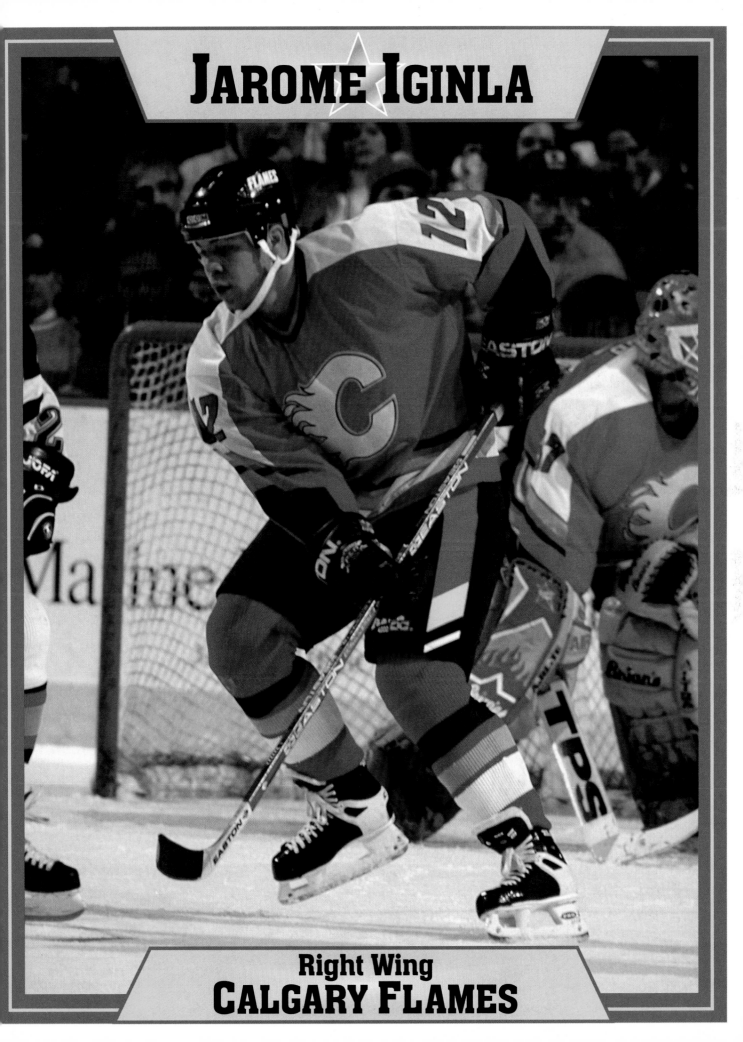

JAROME IGINLA

Right Wing
CALGARY FLAMES

SAKU KOIVU
Montreal Canadiens

Montreal teams of the past are legendary. In the good old days of the game, the Canadiens played what fans liked to call "firewagon hockey." Players like Maurice "The Rocket" Richard, Bernie "Boom Boom" Geoffrion and, more recently, Guy Lafleur were nicknamed "The Flying Frenchmen," a tribute to their fast-paced, offensive style.

In comparison, recent Montreal teams have been less thrilling to watch. Rather than hitting their opponents with an explosive offence, they've been trying to play it safe with sound defence.

But last season the Canadiens decided to tip back the scale and bring back some of the old excitement. Leading the return to the wild days of "The Flying Frenchmen" was none other than "The Flying Finn," Saku Koivu.

"Saku reminds me in some ways of Henri Richard," says Montreal General Manager Rejean Houle. "He's quick and he has great talent and enthusiasm. He's a special player."

"He's the kind of guy who you explain something to once and then he understands," says former Montreal coach Jacques Demers. "He won't make the same mistake three or four times once you show him how to do it."

Saku had a respectable rookie season, finishing up with 20 goals and 25 assists for 45 points. Last season he tallied 56 points, despite playing in only 50 games because of injuries.

For a fast, deft player like Saku, last year's offensive style fit like a glove. But the Canadiens's new strategy brought mixed results. They were exciting to watch, but had trouble keeping the puck out of their net at times.

"I was feeling very comfortable last season," he says. "It's more the kind of hockey I used to play in Finland. I know we have to improve our defensive play, though. You have to have both to be successful."

Fans will be keeping a close eye on Saku and the Canadiens this year. If they can balance their new, entertaining style with an equally strong defence, they could be invincible.

STATS
Saku Koivu

- Montreal's 1st pick (21st overall) 1993 NHL Entry Draft
- First NHL Team & Season — Montreal Canadiens 1995–96
- Born — November 23, 1974, in Turku, Finland
- Position — Center
- Shoots — Left
- Height — 1.75 m (5'9")
- Weight — 81 kg (180 lbs.)

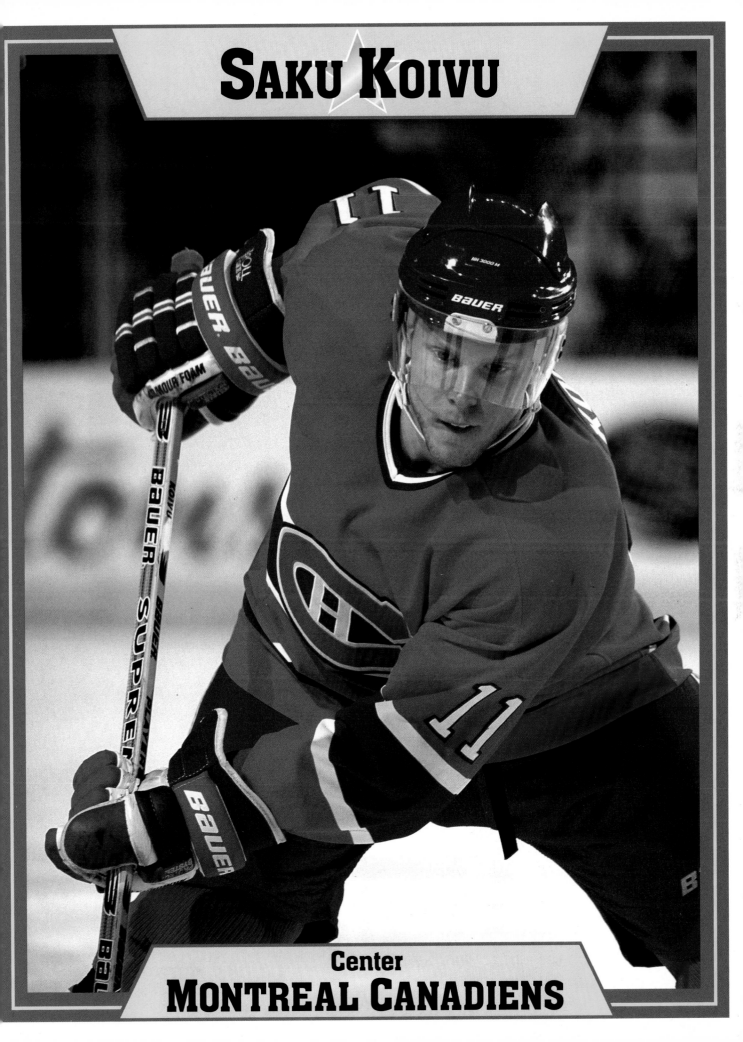

SAKU KOIVU

Center
MONTREAL CANADIENS

ERIC LINDROS
Philadelphia Flyers

To many hockey fans, Eric Lindros represents the finest combination of physical strength and skill in the game. Some nights, it's almost as though he should be playing in his own league.

Now that Mario Lemieux has retired, could Eric be the best player in the game? That can be tough to judge. First of all, you won't get an answer out of him.

"That's not what I'm about," he says. "I just go out and do my thing and hope that the team does well. If other people want to talk about who's better at this or that, then that's for them to do."

Next: along with strength and skill, a player needs to have good instincts. Some feel Jaromir Jagr has the best feel for the game, but lately Eric has been playing with real finesse.

"I think maybe two or three years ago you could have said that Eric wasn't as creative offensively as some of the best," says Philadelphia coach Terry Murray. "But in the last couple of seasons Eric has become much less predictable and much more creative with the puck. He doesn't just run through people with it anymore."

Another way to judge a player is to look at the effect he has on his peers. The truly great players are leaders, inspiring teammates with a positive attitude and work ethic, on the ice and off. Eric scores points there, too.

"This is much more of Eric's club than it was before," says Murray. "[His] leadership in the room has really emerged."

And few players in the NHL are quicker to share success and praise with their teammates than Eric. Though he's often the big scoring star of a game, afterward he always makes sure that everyone knows who set him up.

"It's a team game," he says. "It's good to be aggressive and to score goals and have success, but it's a mistake to think that you can do it all on your own. When we win it's because everyone is working well together for the same thing."

Is Eric next in line for the "best in the game" title? *You* decide.

STATS
Eric Lindros

- Quebec's 1st pick (1st overall) 1991 NHL Entry Draft
- First NHL Team & Season — Philadelphia Flyers 1992–93
- Born — February 28, 1973, in London, Ontario
- Position — Center
- Shoots — Right
- Height — 1.93 m (6'4")
- Weight — 106 kg (236 lbs.)

ERIC LINDROS

Center
PHILADELPHIA FLYERS

PATRICK ROY
Colorado Avalanche

Though he once seemed destined to be a lifelong Montreal Canadien, Patrick Roy is now very much at home in his third year with the Colorado Avalanche. At the age of 31, he's playing as well as ever — or better.

"Not only is he a great goalie," says his coach Marc Crawford, "but he also brings a tremendous presence to the dressing room as a leader. Patrick has tremendous personality on and off the ice."

Some might call that cockiness or overconfidence, but the truth is, on the ice, Patrick always proves himself right — especially in the most pressure-filled, important games. Players refer to it as "delivering the goods."

What really makes him tick is his desire to be the best — of this season, and of all time. He hit two career records last year, with 38 wins and a 2.32 goals-against average. Patrick already has more playoff wins than any other goaltender and, if he plays long enough, he could take a run at Terry Sawchuk's all-time career-win total of 447.

"I want to be the best, of course," he says. "You have to think that way to play goal in this league. When I'm confident I'm hard to beat."

In his last days with Montreal two seasons ago, the fans could detect a nick or two in Patrick's armor of confidence. He wasn't his usual sharp self. Some nights, his play was utterly ordinary. But all that changed after his trade to the Avalanche. He had a tremendous run of success in the 1996 playoffs, and wound up helping to bring home Colorado's first Stanley Cup.

"A big part of it was that I was having fun again," recalls Patrick. "I loved my time in Montreal, but the last couple of years there I wasn't having as much fun. When you can't go to the rink and enjoy the game and being with the guys, then there's something wrong.

"It's funny how things change, isn't it? At one time I could never have imagined playing for any other team than the Montreal Canadiens. And now it seems like it was a long time ago. All in all, the change did me good."

STATS
Patrick Roy

- Montreal's 4th pick (51st overall) 1984 NHL Entry Draft
- First NHL Team & Season — Montreal Canadiens 1985–86
- Born — October 5, 1965, in Quebec City, Quebec
- Position — Goaltender
- Shoots — Left
- Height — 1.83 m (6')
- Weight — 86.5 kg (192 lbs.)

PATRICK ROY

Goal
COLORADO AVALANCHE

JOE SAKIC
Colorado Avalanche

The greatest players in the game follow their instincts. They can judge the way a play will unfold and position themselves where they can do the most good. Just watch the way Wayne Gretzky finds the open man for a pass, or Jaromir Jagr takes the shortest route to the front of the opponent's net. They have the feel.

Joe Sakic, the Colorado Avalanche's outstanding forward, has it too.

"That's the way I've always tried to be," he says. "I like to read the play and react on it. I've found that while I'm struggling, I tend to think too much about what it is I want to do, rather than just reading and reacting."

But instinct isn't everything. Joe has put in his fair share of hard work, too. When he first arrived in the NHL his skating was weak. He didn't have explosive speed — the kind a player needs when chasing the puck or trying to find open ice. But he was aware of this shortcoming and corrected it with an intense weightlifting program.

The combination of instinct and speed has made Joe one of the most dangerous offensive players of this decade. He has exceeded 100 points in a season five times, and led his team in scoring for seven of the last eight seasons. On the franchise's list of all-time scorers, Joe is third — and he's the only one of the top three still playing for the club.

But for all his personal achievements, Joe didn't receive much recognition until his team made headlines. When Colorado won the 1996 Stanley Cup it marked a coming-out party, of sorts, for Joe.

"There is no greater satisfaction than being part of a team that wins the Cup," says Joe. "From the time you are a kid playing street hockey with your buddies, you dream of scoring the big goal and winning it all. There is nothing I have done that has given me more satisfaction than being part of that team the first time we won it."

STATS
Joe Sakic

- Quebec's 2nd pick (15th overall) 1987 NHL Entry Draft
- First NHL Team & Season — Quebec Nordiques 1988–89
- Born — July 7, 1969, in Burnaby, British Columbia
- Position — Center
- Shoots — Left
- Height — 1.80 m (5'11")
- Weight — 83 kg (185 lbs.)

JOE SAKIC

Center
COLORADO AVALANCHE

TEEMU SELANNE
Mighty Ducks of Anaheim

On the ice, Teemu Selanne, the "Finnish Flash," is one of the fastest and most exciting players in the NHL. But while at home in Finland, he lives up to his nickname behind the wheel of a finely tuned car.

"The skills of rally racing are very similar to those in hockey," he says. "You need to have good reactions, you have to concentrate and you need good focus. Sometimes it will be a three-day rally, with you and your partner in the car for many hours at a time. You have to be in good shape and you have to keep your concentration. It can be really tough, but that's why it's fun."

Having fun is a big part of Teemu's life. In many ways he's like a kid in a grownup's body. So it isn't surprising to learn that he loves children and even once taught kindergarten.

"It's something I really enjoyed, working with the kids," he says. "They're so excited about things and are fun to be around."

Today, Teemu involves himself in children's charities. He was recently named "first godfather" — an honorary title — to the Children's Hospital of Finland. He also coaches young players at a Helsinki hockey school during the off-season.

For Teemu, giving his time is a matter of principle.

"We are all so lucky to be able to do what we're doing, playing hockey in the NHL for a living," he says. "People like Wayne Gretzky and Jari Kurri, they know how important the fans and the kids are. I try to be like them. It takes some effort to do these things but it is important to people."

The Mighty Ducks of Anaheim may not yet be serious contenders, but they already have a solid foundation in players like Paul Kariya and Teemu. And the Finnish Flash is confident that his team will achieve success.

"Our team will get better," says Teemu. "You wait and see. We need to work hard and good things will happen."

In the meantime, he and his teammates will ensure that Ducks fans enjoy plenty of thrilling action.

STATS
Teemu Selanne

- Winnipeg's 1st pick (10th overall) 1988 NHL Entry Draft
- First NHL Team & Season — Winnipeg Jets 1992–93
- Born — July 3, 1970, in Helsinki, Finland
- Position — Right Wing
- Shoots — Right
- Height — 1.83 m (6')
- Weight — 90 kg (200 lbs.)

TEEMU SELANNE

Right Wing
MIGHTY DUCKS OF ANAHEIM

BRENDAN SHANAHAN
Detroit Red Wings

While every hockey player is affected by his emotions to a degree, some are driven by the highs and lows, while others try to play them down and take a businesslike approach. You can put Brendan Shanahan in the first group. He finds that channeling his emotions makes him a better player.

"I'm definitely an emotional player," says Brendan. "I play better when I'm emotional. But to play with that emotion you have to fight some battles, experience life in the trenches — some wins and losses — before you get to that special feeling of wanting to play for the logo on the front of the sweater and the other guys who are wearing it."

In his 10 seasons with the NHL, Brendan has played for four different teams. He started with the New Jersey Devils, then after four seasons became a free agent with St. Louis. Four years later he played for Hartford for a year, then was traded to Detroit. He is now in his second season with the Red Wings.

"It was tough leaving St. Louis at the time," Brendan recalls. "I thought we had a good team and that we were moving toward putting it all together and winning the Cup. As it turns out, that didn't happen, for a number of reasons. But it seemed like we were getting close there.

"I had the same feeling when I arrived in Detroit: being part of a team that has all the ingredients. At this point in my career I've enjoyed all of the great things that this business can bring you. But for me . . . what I'm in it for is to win the Cup."

An impulsive guy like Brendan likes to have a laugh now and then — and he has been known to stretch the truth a little. Among his past occupations listed in team guide books are "lifeguard," "backup goaltender for Ireland's World Cup soccer team" and "extra in the movie *Forrest Gump*"! Quite a resume for one of the best power forwards in hockey.

It's just another case of Brendan keeping people on their toes — as he does his opponents.

STATS
Brendan Shanahan

- New Jersey's 1st pick (2nd overall) 1987 NHL Entry Draft
- First NHL Team & Season — New Jersey Devils 1987–88
- Born — January 23, 1969, in Mimico, Ontario
- Position — Left Wing
- Shoots — Right
- Height — 1.90 m (6'3")
- Weight — 98 kg (218 lbs.)

BRENDAN SHANAHAN

Left Wing
DETROIT RED WINGS

MATS SUNDIN
Toronto Maple Leafs

A bad season can really test the character of a team and its players.

Last year presented such a test to the Toronto Maple Leafs and their star forward, Mats Sundin. Despite Mats's performance as one of the top offensive players in the NHL, the season was a struggle for the Leafs.

"The most frustrating thing," said Mats last season, "is that we have so much experience on this team. We have guys who have been around the league for years. We should be doing so much better."

Spirits were high among Toronto fans as the team headed into the season with a bright new coach, Mike Murphy, and a cast of veteran players including Doug Gilmour, Kirk Muller and Larry Murphy. And expectations were high that younger players like Felix Potvin and Mats Sundin would continue to develop their talents.

Mats had high expectations, too.

"I wanted to bring my game up another notch last season," he says. "I felt great from the start of the season coming off of the World Cup experience with Sweden. I was looking forward to a big season."

While some of his teammates complained that they felt sluggish after the tournament, Mats used it as a springboard for success. The Leafs fought an uphill battle all the way, but Mats emerged as a true superstar, finishing seventh in league scoring, with 41 goals and 53 assists for 94 points.

Now coming into the prime of his hockey career, Mats longs for his team to be competitive enough to take a run at the Stanley Cup.

"I played in Quebec the first few years of my career and we struggled. We only made the playoffs one year," recalls Mats. "I don't really want to have to go through that again. This is such a great hockey city. The people in Toronto support the team even when it's losing. It would be great for the fans if we could give them a winner."

Mats has shown his true character — he's survived a tough year with his spirits still high. Will the Maple Leafs bounce back? Fans will have to wait and watch.

STATS
Mats Sundin

- Quebec's 1st pick (1st overall) 1989 NHL Entry Draft
- First NHL Team & Season — Quebec Nordiques 1990–91
- Born — February 13, 1971, in Edmonton, Alberta
- Position — Center/Right Wing
- Shoots — Right
- Height — 1.93 m (6'4")
- Weight — 97 kg (215 lbs.)

MATS SUNDIN

Center/Right Wing
TORONTO MAPLE LEAFS

OLEG TVERDOVSKY
Phoenix Coyotes

The hockey world often expects too much too soon from some of its great young prospects.

Take the case of Phoenix defenceman Oleg Tverdovsky. Drafted second overall in the 1994 Entry Draft by the Mighty Ducks of Anaheim, Oleg was pegged to be a leader for the new and developing team. One NHL scout even said he could be "as great as Bobby Orr." It was all just a bit much for a player who hadn't even played his first game in the NHL.

"It made me very uncomfortable," says Oleg, "to be compared to the greatest player ever to play the game. I knew there would be high expectations but I didn't think they'd be quite so high."

One of the problems he had in Anaheim was adjusting to the style of play being promoted by his coach at the time, Ron Wilson. Though Oleg had been drafted as an offensive defenceman, Wilson wanted him to concentrate more on defence.

"I guess they were worried that I would make too many mistakes if I played an offensive style. I respect what the coach was trying to do, but that was not the system for me."

When he was finally traded, Oleg found happiness.

"Last year in Phoenix I was able to do what I do best. The coach [Don Hay] was giving me lots of ice time, and I believe that helped me settle into our system here and make more of a contribution."

With Phoenix, Oleg saw regular duty on the power play, as well as in even-strength situations. He led the Coyotes defencemen in scoring, finishing with 10 goals and 45 assists for 55 points. His teammates were especially impressed by Oleg's willingness to learn all the facets of the game.

"You can see that he wants to be the best," says Coyotes captain Keith Tkachuk. "You could see how much better he got playing against the best players in the league. He's only 21. . . . I think it's going to be fun watching him develop even more over the next few years."

Coyotes fans will be doing just that.

STATS
Oleg Tverdovsky

- Anaheim's 1st pick (2nd overall) 1994 NHL Entry Draft
- First NHL Team & Season — Mighty Ducks of Anaheim 1994–95
- Born — May 18, 1976, in Donetsk, Russia
- Position — Defence
- Shoots — Left
- Height — 1.83 m (6′)
- Weight — 83 kg (185 lbs.)

OLEG TVERDOVSKY

Defence
PHOENIX COYOTES

JOHN VANBIESBROUCK
Florida Panthers

While most of us in North America have to tough it out through the winter, in Florida even the worst days usually feel balmy.

The climate there may have helped John Vanbiesbrouck's playing since he joined the Florida Panthers four years ago. Or maybe "Beezer," as his teammates call him, has simply hit his peak as a goalie.

"He is a bona fide top goaltender and he's at the top of his game," says Panthers coach Doug MacLean. "Over the years he's had to fight through some hard times. He's faced questions as to whether or not he could play pressure hockey down the stretch and into the playoffs. I think he's more than answered those questions."

John will always be remembered for the string of electrifying games he put together in the 1996 Stanley Cup playoffs. Though the Panthers were defeated in the final that year, John was at his absolute best. His greatest effort was in game four, the 1-0 triple overtime that clinched the Cup for Colorado. John faced 56 shots!

His opponents were awestruck.

"He did things out there that I've never seen before or since," recalls Colorado defenceman Uwe Krupp.

Today, John continues to play a huge role in Florida's success, in more ways than one. What he achieves in the game is clear for all to see, but he's a leader behind the scenes as well.

"His play on the ice gives us confidence," says MacLean. "But he's also well respected off the ice by our guys, because he's been around the league a long time and because of the way he carries himself around fans and the media. He's a true professional."

"My whole career has been a long and winding road," says John. "There have been some bumps along the road, but they've become smoother and easier to handle as time has gone on. I think I've matured as a goalie and a person here in Florida. It's been a great experience for me and my family. I've never seen fans and players as connected as we are here in Florida. I've been here since day one and it's been quite a ride."

STATS
John Vanbiesbrouck

- New York Rangers' 5th pick (72nd overall) 1981 NHL Entry Draft
- First NHL Team & Season — New York Rangers 1983–84
- Born — September 4, 1963, in Detroit, Michigan
- Position — Goaltender
- Shoots — Left
- Height — 1.73 m (5′8″)
- Weight — 79 kg (176 lbs.)

John Vanbiesbrouck

Goal
Florida Panthers

DOUG WEIGHT
Edmonton Oilers

The Edmonton Oilers are quite a story. From 1983–1984 to 1989–1990, they took home five out of seven Stanley Cups. But on the heels of their run as one of the most successful teams in NHL history, everything changed. They became a shadow of their once great selves, finishing out of the playoffs four years in a row.

However, with smart trading and coaching the Oilers have started to bounce back. They even qualified for the playoffs last season, making it clear to fans that the worst was over.

Says Edmonton coach Ron Low, "We have a great bunch of good young players who want to be part of turning this thing around. When I see players like Doug Weight, Jason Arnott, Mariusz Czerkawski and Ryan Smyth, I know the future is bright."

Doug Weight has certainly come into his own. He led his team in scoring for the last two seasons, finishing last year with 21 goals and 61 assists for 82 points. For him, the secret to success is in believing the team can do it.

"You look around the dressing room at the core of guys who have been here for the last three or four years," says Weight, "and you can see the confidence starting to come."

Doug first caught people's attention at the 1991 World Junior Hockey Championship. Playing for Team USA, he led the tournament in scoring with 19 points. He then spent two seasons with the New York Rangers, and showed potential on the team. But in the end he was traded to Edmonton in exchange for Esa Tikkanen.

"Of course I wish I could have done a little more with the Rangers," recalls Doug. "As it turns out, though, this was a great move for me. I'm on the first line here and get lots of playing time. I've gained more confidence and become a better player in the last four seasons."

The entire Oilers team has improved along with Doug, and fans are expecting great things from them. The test will be whether Doug and his teammates can raise their game yet another notch this season and meet those expectations.

STATS
Doug Weight

- New York Rangers' 2nd pick (34th overall) 1990 NHL Entry Draft
- First NHL Team & Season — New York Rangers 1990–91
- Born — January 21, 1971, in Warren, Michigan
- Position — Center
- Shoots — Left
- Height — 1.80 m (5'11")
- Weight — 86 kg (191 lbs.)

DOUG ★ WEIGHT

Center
EDMONTON OILERS

DO YOU KNOW. . .?

1. Daniel Alfredsson won the Calder Trophy as the NHL's rookie of the year in 1996. The previous year's award also went to a Swedish player. Who was it?

2. Most of Wayne Gretzky's professional hockey career goals have been scored for NHL teams. How many regular-season goals did he score as a player in the World Hockey Association?

3. What superstitious ritual does Colorado Avalanche goalie Patrick Roy follow before every game?

4. Name the two oldest arenas currently in use in the NHL.

5. Name the only player ever to have had his name misspelled on the Stanley Cup.

6. Which NHL team missed the playoffs last season — for the first time since 1966–67?

7. Name the youngest player ever to score 100 points in an NHL season.

---

1. Peter Forsberg of the Quebec Nordiques.

2. Wayne scored 46 regular-season goals in the now-defunct league: 3 for the Indianapolis Racers and 43 for the Edmonton Oilers.

3. He writes the names of his three kids — Jonathan, Frederick and Jana — on his hockey stick.

4. Toronto's Maple Leaf Gardens, built in 1931, and Pittsburgh's Civic Arena, built in 1961.

5. Adam Deadmarsh, a member of the 1996 Colorado Avalanche. His name was incorrectly spelled "Deadmarch," but has since been re-engraved.

6. The Boston Bruins. Last year marked the end of a 29-season run for the team.

7. Dale Hawerchuk. He was a month shy of his 19th birthday when he registered his 100th point of the 1981–82 season, playing for the Winnipeg Jets.

The All-Star Game

About halfway through the season there is an All-Star game played in one NHL city. The game features the All-Stars from the Western Conference against the All-Stars from the Eastern Conference.

   Fill this in right after you watch the game on television.

Date of game: _____Jan. 18_____   Where was it played? _____Vancouver_____

Winning team: _____North   America_____

Final score: _____8-7_____

The winning goal was scored by: _____

Most valuable player of the game (MVP): _____Teemu   Selanne_____

Highlights of the Game

The following players scored:

_____   _____

_____   _____

_____   _____

_____

The best play of the game was when: _____

_____

The best save was when: _____

_____

Other highlights: _____

_____

_____

_____

Penalties

Do you know what is happening when the referee stops play and makes a penalty call? If you don't, then you're missing an important part of the game. The referee can call different penalties that result in everything from playing a man short for two minutes to having a player kicked out of the game.

Here are some of the most common referee signals. Now you'll know what penalties are being called against your team.

Boarding
Pounding the closed fist of one hand into the open palm of the other hand.

Charging
Rotating clenched fists around one another in front of the chest.

Cross-checking
A forward and backward motion with both fists clenched extending from the chest.

Elbowing
Tapping the elbow of the "whistle hand" with the opposite hand.

High-sticking
Holding both fists, clenched, one above the other.

Holding
Clasping the wrist of the "whistle hand" well in front of the chest.

Hooking
A tugging motion with both arms, as if pulling something toward the stomach.

Roughing
A thrusting motion with the arm extending from the side.

Interference
Crossed arms stationary in front of the chest with fists closed.

Slashing
A chopping motion with the edge of one hand across the opposite forearm.

Tripping
Striking the right leg with the right hand below the knee while keeping both skates on the ice.

Wash-out
Both arms swung laterally across the body with palms facing down. Used by the referee, it means no goal.

Spearing
A jabbing motion with both hands thrust out in front of the body.

Unsportsmanlike conduct
Use both hands to form a "T" in front of the chest.

Your Own Hockey Career

Whether you play in a league, at school, or just for recreation, it's fun to keep track of how you and your team do during the season.

This section is for you to fill in with the details of your hockey career — both the high points and the low points.

Your team's name: _____

Name of the league: _____

Position you play: _____

Your team nickname: _____

Some of the other players on the team:

_____   _____

_____   _____

_____   _____

_____   _____

_____   _____

_____   _____

_____   _____

Season Highlights
The most exciting game you played in this season was: _____

_____

_____

Your own best game was: _____

_____

_____

_____

The best team you played against this season was: _____

_____

The closest game you played was: _____

_____

Your worst game was: _____

_____

_____

The funniest thing that happened to you during a hockey game this season was:

_____

_____

Here's your own personal score sheet — fill this out after every game.

	OTHER TEAM	GOALS	ASSISTS	POINTS
GAME #1				
GAME #2				
GAME #3				
GAME #4				
GAME #5				
GAME #6				
GAME #7				
GAME #8				
GAME #9				
GAME #10				

The Stanley Cup Playoffs

The Stanley Cup Playoffs start in April and usually run until the end of May. Before reaching the final, teams must first win their respective Division and Conference championships.

Keep track below:

Pacific Division Champion: _____

Central Division Champion: _____

Western Conference Champion: _____

Atlantic Division Champion: _____

Northeast Division Champion: _____

Eastern Division Champion: _____

Stanley Cup Final

Which two teams played? _____

Who won? _____

How many games did the series go to? _____

Who was the Playoff MVP? _____

Clip a picture from the newspaper of the winning team
with the Stanley Cup after the final game. Tape the picture below.

The Final — Game-by-Game

Fill out this part of your record keeper after each game of the
Stanley Cup Final while you can still feel the excitement!
Fill in the final score, where the game was played, who scored
and any other information you can think of.

GAME
1

GAME
2

GAME
3

GAME
4

GAME
5

GAME
6

GAME
7

NHL Awards

Here are some of the major NHL awards for individual players. Fill in your selection for each award and then fill in the name of the actual winner of the trophy.

HART MEMORIAL TROPHY

Awarded to the player judged to be the most valuable to his team. Selected by the Professional Hockey Writers Association.

Your choice: _Jaromir Jagr_   The winner: _____

ART ROSS TROPHY

Awarded to the player who leads the league in scoring points at the end of the regular season.

Your choice: _Jaromir Jagr_   The winner: _____

CALDER MEMORIAL TROPHY

Awarded to the player selected as the most proficient in his first year of competition in the NHL. Selected by the Professional Hockey Writers Association.

Your choice: _Sergei Samsonov_   The winner: _____

JAMES NORRIS TROPHY

Awarded to the defence player who demonstrates throughout his season the greatest all-round ability. Selected by the Professional Hockey Writers Association.

Your choice: _Nicklas Lidstrom_   The winner: _____

VEZINA TROPHY

Awarded to the goalkeeper judged to be the best. Selected by the NHL general managers.

Your choice: _Martin Brodeur_   The winner: _____